COCKTAILS

EXPERIMENTATIONS OF A TWISTED MIND

KEITH NICHOLAS

Published by Keith Nicholas

ISBN: 978-0-6457942-0-5

First edition, 2023

For enquiries, contact:
knic0067@bigpond.net.au

A catalogue record for this book is available from the National Library of Australia

NATIONAL LIBRARY OF AUSTRALIA

CONTENTS

INTRODUCTION

For me cocktails are more than something that you have on special occasions with friends. They are a way of being creative, adventurous, and sometimes very surprising. Creating cocktails is an escape, a way of letting go of the troubles of the week, bringing back a little sanity where there is often chaos.

I have been very lucky to have a local hotel that has employed several outstanding mixologists over the years, and having a reasonably good palate, they would use me as a testing opportunity for their new creations. The resulting collaboration between staff and myself in refining the cocktails was both a great learning experience for me and has led to some of the best cocktails coming out of a pub in Adelaide. I am not going to name all the wonderful staff at The Highway in Plympton, South Australia, who over the years have taught me what it is to invent a cocktail. Many of them patiently followed my directions too, sometimes thinking I was mad, maybe they are right, and assisted me to develop the creations of which a small number have been replicated in this book. Without those people and the understanding of the hotel management this book probably would never have come to be.

This book isn't just recipes for some of the cocktails I've created, it's also about why they were created in the first place.

This is a portion of the experiments I've created, and new ones are occurring regularly. You never know; if this book is successful some other cocktails might make it into a second edition.

SYRUPS

Most cocktails need a syrup or straight sugar. Syrups can be a cheap and excellent way to enhance the flavour of the cocktail. I've included recipes for the ones used in this book or you can just look for ready-made versions and buy them.

Simple Syrup

1 cup water
1 cup sugar

Put water in saucepan and bring water to the boil, dissolve the sugar in the water stirring constantly. Once sugar has dissolved reduce heat, cover, and simmer for 5-10 minutes. Remove pan from heat and allow contents to cool completely, then bottle.

Ginger Syrup

1 ½ cups water
1 cup white sugar
¼ cup coarsely chopped unpeeled fresh ginger
½ teaspoon whole black peppercorns
2 tablespoons freshly squeezed lemon juice

Mix together water, sugar, ginger, lemon juice, and peppercorns in a saucepan. Bring to a boil; reduce heat and simmer, stirring frequently, until sugar dissolves. Let cool, 15 to 30 minutes. Strain syrup through a fine-mesh sieve; discard solids. Chill, covered, for up to 2 weeks.

Mint Syrup

1 cup water
1 cup white sugar
1 cup fresh mint leaves

Combine water, sugar, and mint leaves in a small saucepan. Bring to a boil, stirring until sugar dissolves. Simmer for 1 minute. Remove from heat and let syrup steep, about 30 minutes. Pour syrup into a sterilized glass jar through a mesh strainer to remove mint leaves; let cool.

Passionfruit Syrup

4 ripe passion fruit (ripe passion fruit are very wrinkly)
½ cup water   ½ cup sugar

In a small saucepan, bring water and sugar to a boil. Stir until the sugar is dissolved and remove from heat. Add the passion fruit pulp into the simple syrup. Stir and let the passion fruit steep for about 2 hours. Place a fine mesh sieve over a glass measuring cup and pour the contents of the saucepan through the sieve. Do not press on the seeds if you want the simple syrup to be clear.

Allspice Syrup

1 cup sugar   1 cup water
1 tablespoon allspice berries

In a spice grinder, coarsely grind the allspice berries. In a small saucepan, combine the ground allspice with the water and bring to a boil. Remove from the heat, cover and let stand for 20 minutes. Pour through a fine strainer into a jar. Add the sugar, cover and shake gently until dissolved. Refrigerate for up to 1 month.

COCKTAILS

Each cocktail has a story...

Sometimes it's a theme I want to follow. Sometimes it's an ingredient or a flavour that I'm trying to achieve. Sometimes I'm just looking for a slightly twisted flavour of a classic. Occasionally what I want comes on the first attempt; often it takes multiple attempts of minor twists to get the exact flavour I'm looking for. Sometimes an experiment doesn't produce what I started looking for but what results is pretty good in its own right.

You may notice there's a limited palette of ingredients and often commonality in the fruit used, which is due to the fact they are all made in one bar, and I'm limited by what they have on hand. There is no special ordering of unique ingredients here. Whilst some of these cocktails look pretty and often the garnishes are from the bar staff, my main objective is how the cocktails taste. Because no special ingredients or tools means anyone with little experience can recreate these at home. And you can put your own twists on them. Isn't that what making cocktails is all about anyway?

Where possible, I have listed alternatives that will give you close to the flavours I achieved in the recipe as written.

A warning to all, some of my cocktails tend to be a little heavy on the alcohol, so moderation is the key.

4

PINK GIN MARTINI

The Story and Tasting

This cocktail was one of the first I invented, so it gets pride of place as the first in the book. I was trying to get that wonderful pale pink colour. What I produced was a wonderful, easy drinking summer cocktail.

What you should taste is a slightly citrus flavour, less sweet than a cosmopolitan with, what I believe is a better colour.

Ingredients

45 ml gin
15 ml lime juice
60 apple juice
15 ml cranberry
15 ml sugar syrup

Method

Add all ingredients into a shaker, add ice and shake, strain into chilled martini glass. Garnish with mint sprig.

SPB

SMOKEY PEACH BOURBON OR PEACHY APPLE RYE

The Story and Tasting

Also known as Peachy Apply Rye.

A real labour of love and the first time I truly put my knowledge of flavours to the test. It works best with a slightly smoked rye bourbon. Peach, bourbon, and apple are just ingredients that are meant to be together.

A light refreshing drink – you will probably want to have more than one. If you use a smoky or peated whiskey, then expect a slight tang on the aftertaste.

Ingredients

30 ml rye bourbon
(preferably smoky)
15 ml peach schnapps
5 ml mint syrup
45 ml apple juice

Method

Put all ingredients into a shaker with ice and shake. Strain into chilled martini glass with a mint leaf garnish.

MOCHA OLD FASHIONED

The Story and Tasting

I love an old fashioned, I also love coffee and chocolate. So, when the bar got some chocolate bitters and a good coffee liquor, some twisting of a favourite was definitely on the cards.

Done right this is a wonderful balance of alcohol, coffee, and chocolate. Slightly sweeter than a traditional old fashioned. I'll give warning that it's much easier to drink than a traditional but just as potent.

Ingredients

45 ml scotch or bourbon or dark rum (smoothest available)
15 ml Mr Black Coffee Liqueur
Sugar syrup
Chocolate bitters
or
10 ml chocolate liqueur

Method

Build as per old fashioned in a tumbler. Garnish with cherries.

TEQUILA LIME DROP

The Story and Tasting

As all good cocktails begin, this came about because of the tequila; very light, easy drinking and refreshing. A very citrusy tart drink that will probably limit you to only one.

Great to have between courses to cleanse your palate.

Ingredients

30 ml Casamigos tequila
(or another good tequila)
30 ml Cointreau
10 ml lemonade
Juice of half a Fresh lime

Method

Shake and serve in chilled martini glass.
A twist on a lemon drop using tequila instead of gin or vodka.

SPICED GINGER SOUR

The Story and Tasting

I know many people love fireball especially as a shot, personally I don't. I do like cinnamon and ginger. So, after a few attempts I came up with this particular cocktail which makes drinking fireball bearable.

You should get a good mix of cinnamon, ginger and almond; almost like an apple pie with meringue.

Ingredients

45 ml Fireball
15 ml Disaronno or another almond/hazelnut liqueur
25 ml ginger syrup
60 ml apple juice
Egg white

Method

Put all ingredients in a shaker and dry shake with egg white. Add ice and re-shake. Serve in tumbler over ice.

MANHATTAN HONEY

The Story and Tasting

This one started because I was drinking a traditional Manhattan and a friend asked to try it, they found it too bitter and alcoholic (their words not mine).

As it happened, the bar had recently got in some American Honey Bourbon. Wow! What a transformation just replacing normal whiskey.

This is smooth and slightly sweet with that beautiful ruby colour. I almost like this more than the traditional (almost).

Ingredients

60 ml American honey bourbon
30 ml vermouth (rosa)
5 drops bitters
3 spoons cherry juice
1 maraschino cherry

Method

Stir all ingredients except cherry with ice. Place cherry in martini glass. Strain ingredients into glass.

NEGRONI BLANCO

The Story and Tasting

As you would have guessed, nothing in cocktail making is sacred to me; even the negroni, everything old needs a new twist.

A traditional negroni is a wonderful thing, the perfect balance of vermouth, Campari and gin.

However, sometimes I want something a little different. This one is definitely heavy on the alcohol, so take it easy and sip slowly, it will actually mellow as the ice melts.

This should taste less bitter than the traditional negroni and is much easier to drink before the ice melts.

Ingredients

30 ml gin
30 ml limoncello or triple sec
30 ml white vermouth
Optional dash of lemonade if you want a cloudier look

Method

Add ingredients to glass, and stir with ice, then strain into a tumbler with fresh ice. (Preferred large single ice cube).

VODKA CITRUS

The Story and Tasting

A twist on the tequila lime drop, except using vodka. You could also use lemons, but make sure you pick ones that are really sour.

It has a bit of tang, mixed with sweetness of the lemonade and sugar, very refreshing and easy drinking, but be careful – too many could be a problem.

Ingredients

30 ml vodka
30 ml Cointreau
30 ml lemonade
Juice of one lime
10 ml sugar syrup

Method

Shake with ice and strain into martini glass.

A warning make sure your shaker is tight on, mishaps can occur when shaking carbonated liquids like lemonade.

STRAWBERRY SPRITZ

The Story and Tasting

This one came about when trying to find a truly summery drink. The addition of a little lemonade or soda before shaking adds a sparkle and cloudiness to the result. Be careful to ensure the shaker is really sealed before you start.

You should certainly taste strawberries, but the hint of peach and lemon from the liquors ought to really brighten up your pallet.

Ingredients

3 muddled strawberries
30 ml Cointreau
30 ml peach vodka
10 ml berry puree
Dash lemonade

Method

Put all items into shaker with ice and shake. Strain into wine glass and add ice. Garnish with strawberry.

COCONUT FRUITY

The Story and Tasting

Along come coconut flavoured sprits – in this case tequila. When the tequila ran out, we substituted rum, not quite the same but close. This should have a taste similar to a Pina Colada.

Ingredients

Pineapple piece
Lychee
45 ml 1800 coconut tequila or coconut flavoured rum
15 ml passionfruit liqueur
15 ml lime juice
15 ml agave

Method

Muddle fruit with agave, add tequila/ rum, lime, and liqueur. Shake, strain over ice in a tumbler and garnish with dehydrated pineapple.

SUMMER MARTINI

The Story and Tasting

So many summer fruits in the fridge, here is one to get them all together. It also scales up wonderfully to make a killer punch or jug.

This is just so tasty, with all that fruit and tropical sweetness and so quick to drink, that you can't stop at one.

Ingredients

2 pieces lychee
2 pieces pineapple
2 strawberries
15 ml peach schnapps
30 ml peach vodka

Method

Muddle fruit then add alcohol. Shake and double strain into a martini glass. Garnish with a fresh strawberry.

RASPBERRY ANISE MARTINI

The Story and Tasting

This was a challenge set by a friend, who didn't think a cocktail using sambuca would work. After a bit of internet searching, I discovered that raspberries, gin and sambuca seemed popular. A bit of experimentation and this is the combination that tastes great.

If you love aniseed flavours this one's going to impress. If liquorice is not your thing, give it a try, it will surprise you.

Ingredients

4 raspberries, plus extra for garnish
2 basil leaves
15 ml lime juice
15 ml orange juice

30 ml gin
10 ml simple syrup
10 ml white sambuca

Method

In a cocktail shaker, muddle the raspberries and basil leaves. Add the lime juice, orange juice, gin, simple syrup, sambuca, and ice. Shake until the cocktail is blended and cold. Strain into a martini glass. Garnish with a raspberry.

PEARYDELICIOUS

The Story and Tasting

One Thursday, they had some pears behind the bar, so I created this one. It was nice to use something other than berries and tropical fruits. This is a great summer drink; unfortunately, fresh pears are only available in winter. Very refreshing, subtle flavours.

Ingredients

Pineapple slice
Pear slice
15 ml Cointreau
45 ml gin (citrus flavour)
30 ml apple juice
60 ml pineapple juice
Splash sugar syrup

Method

Muddle pineapple and pear. Add all the liquids to the muddled fruit with ice and shake. Strain into tumbler with ice. Garnish with pear slice.

BUBBLE GUM BOURBON

The Story and Tasting

This one is a bit unusual. I haven't heard of anyone putting grape liqueur and bourbon together and I wasn't confident that the flavours would be right. Wow was I wrong – all those childhood memories of grape bubble gum came flooding back.

As the name suggests it has flavours reminiscent of grape bubble gum, which in my book is a pretty good flavour.

Ingredients

45 ml Wild Turkey
15 ml Pavan Liqueur
15 ml lemon juice
10 ml sugar syrup
Dash bitters

Method

Shake with ice and serve in tall glass, top with lemonade.

PINEAPPLE PASSION

The Story and tasting

This one looks similar to the *Bubble Gum Bourbon*, but as you can imagine with the altered ingredients smells and tastes very different. A cocktail created to match pineapple rum with passionfruit, the apple juice is a neutral flavour I use to bulk up drinks, so that you get the real taste of the main ingredients.

This should taste very tropical and refreshing, and not as much alcohol as some of my other cocktails so you can smash plenty.

Ingredients

60 ml plantation pineapple rum
60 ml apple juice
30 ml passionfruit syrup
Orange bitters

Method

Shake, serve in tumbler with mint and ice. Garnish with dehydrated apple or pineapple and fresh mint.

SLAP MARTINI

The Story and Tasting

Kangaroo Island Sprits developed a vodka with the flavours of rosemary and olives, that was just made for making into a vodka martini. Alternatively, you could use an olive or savoury flavoured gin.

Not the prettiest cocktail I've ever done, however, it tastes just as you would imagine, a very savoury vodka martini.

Ingredients

Spoon of olive brine
60 ml KIS vodka slap
30 ml mint syrup
15 ml lemon juice
15 ml apple juice

Method

Shake and strain into martini glass with an olive.

SLAPPIN STRAWBERRIES

The Story and Tasting

After I made the slap martini, I started thinking about what other flavours would work. I wasn't sure the savoury taste of the slap vodka would work well with strawberries, however the addition of cracked pepper worked wonderfully.

Savoury, yet sweet and peppery, great with spicy or very rich buttery food.

Ingredients

45 ml KIS vodka slap
2 strawberries
10 ml sugar syrup
10 ml berry syrup
15 ml lime
Cracked pepper

Method

Muddle Strawberries in shaker, add remaining ingredients and shake with ice. Double strain into a martini glass with garnish of strawberry and cracked pepper.

IRIDESCENT MARTINI

The Story and Tasting

This one was all about the colour; I was looking for a sparkly blue. Just the addition of blue curacao didn't work, it wasn't until we added the lemonade that the right opaqueness developed and the cocktail we have here was born.

It tastes of citrus with a little sweetness on the backend. The addition of lemonade makes it sparkly and slightly opaque.

Ingredients

30 ml gin
15 ml blue curacao
30 ml lime juice
15 ml lemonade
10ml sugar syrup

Method

Put all ingredients into a shaker and shake, strain into martini glass. Garnish with a strip of lime zest.

RASPBERRY MARTINI

The Story and Tasting

Lack of ingredients is the mother of all invention. Raspberries were out of season, but I still wanted the raspberry flavours. Luckily the bar got in some raspberry gin and raspberry vodka. I also think the one thing that goes with raspberries (other than anise) is vanilla.

So here it is; a refreshing, slightly sweet martini.

Ingredients

Two lychees
Several mint leaves
30 ml raspberry gin or vodka
15 ml vanilla liqueur (Galliano or Licor 43)
45 ml apple juice

Method

Muddle lychee and mint, add liquids and shake. Double strain into a martini glass.

EGGLESS BLUEBERRY SOUR

The Story and Tasting

This came about because a friend loved the look of sour but couldn't have eggs. This one gives you almost the sour look without the egg danger.

Not a great one to look at but tastes just like a blueberry sour, without quite as much foam.

Ingredients

Blueberries muddled
60 ml Ratu signature rum
30 ml lime juice
10 ml pineapple juice (or chickpea brine)

Method

Put all ingredients into a shaker. Shake, double strain into a tumbler with large ice cube. Garnish with blueberries.

FIJIAN CHOC MANHATTAN

The Story and Tasting

This one isn't mine; it was developed by one of the bartenders from the Highway on his last night just for me. So, thank you Jaimie.

If you love chocolate, this is the drink for you.

Ingredients

45 ml Ratu signature rum
25 ml Antica vermouth
15 ml Mozart Chocolate Liqueur
Choc bitters

Method

Stir all ingredients in a glass with ice, strain into chilled martini glass.

LAKSA MARTINI

The Story and Tasting

One of those truly twisted moments, when you get a bit ambitious and think "can I get the flavours similar to a laksa"? It took a while in my head, and it really came together when Settlers Gin released their Blood Orange and Chilli Gin. This one is spicy, savoury, and I prefer it without the coconut cream. As I said at the beginning of the book, I do have a twisted mind!

Ingredients

45 ml blood orange and chilli gin
5 ml fish sauce optional use extra of olive brine
Fresh coriander
5 ml olive brine
20 ml ginger syrup or liqueur
5 ml lime juice
Lime zest

Optional dash of coconut cream or 10 ml coconut spirit or liqueur.

Method

Put all ingredients in a shaker and shake with ice. Double strain into a chilled martini glass. Garnish with dehydrated lime and coriander leaf.

PINEAPPLE MAI TAI SOUR

The Story and Tasting

This one came about because the bar got in pineapple rum and a former bartender suggested a Mai Tai Sour. So many experiments later, here it is. Unfortunately for everyone allergic to egg, it just doesn't work without the egg white.

Yes, it tastes just like a Mai Tai.

Ingredients

45 ml pineapple rum
30 ml pineapple juice
15 ml lemon/lime
10 ml amaretto / orgeat
egg white

Method

Place all ingredients in shaker, shake for short period to combine then add ice and shake vigorously, strain into a tumbler and garnish with a few drops of bitters and maraschino cherry or grenadine.

SUMMER SPRITZ

The Story and Tasting

Berries and peaches just scream summer. Well, this cocktail combines those with some gin to make a really refreshing drink, just right for those hot summer nights.

Tastes like a really good tropical punch.

Ingredients

2 strawberries (or 6 raspberries) or combination of both
1 lychee
30 ml gin (citrus based)
15 ml peach schnapps
10 ml lime juice
10 ml mint syrup

Method

Muddle fruit together, add other ingredients into shaker. Shake and double strain into pilsner glass, top with Fever Tree Mediterranean Tonic.

PASSIONATE MANGOES

The story and tasting

Another new tequila behind the bar, this one is very citrusy flavour. Passionfruit and mango flavours go in and out comes this little beauty. An excellent drink for those who are not fans of tequila.

Very refreshing, easy drinking.

Ingredients

30 ml Volanda tequila
30 ml Passoa – passionfruit liqueur
45 ml mango puree
10 ml lemon juice

Method

Shake and strain into tumbler and top with lemonade.

GREEN SPICY MARTINI

The Story and Tasting

Similar to the *Laksa Martini*, the inclusion of AGWA gives this a different flavour profile. If I'm completely honest, this is actually even spicier and better than the laksa version.

Spicy and refreshing at the same time, also slightly sweeter than the *Laksa Martini*.

Ingredients

Mint leaves
Cucumber pieces
30 ml AGWA
30 ml Settlers Blood Orange Chilli Gin
15 ml mint syrup
15 ml lime juice
Splash lemonade

Method

Muddle cucumber and mint. Add remaining ingredients. Shake with ice and double strain into a martini glass. Garnish with dehydrated lime and mint leaf.

BLUEBERRY BEACH HOUSE

The Story and Tasting

Beach House Rum has a decidedly vanilla flavour, which enhanced with the Licor 43 and combined with blueberries is a wonderful combination. Because of the vanilla flavours, you could swap the Beach House Rum with another vanilla rum or vodka.

Rum, vanilla, and blueberries – what's not to like?

While you could substitute another vanilla based spiced rum, for me beach house is the only one that works properly.

Ingredients

30 ml Beach House Rum
Blueberries muddled
10 ml Licor 43
60 ml apple juice
10 ml lime juice
Dash mint syrup

Method

Muddle the blueberries, then add remaining ingredients and shake with ice. Double strain into a wine glass and garnish with blueberries.

THE ONE THAT
SHOULDN'T WORK

The Story and Tasting

An experiment where if you looked at the ingredients you would never put them together. Stuck for ideas, we looked at what was behind the bar that hadn't been used in a while. Out comes vermouth, blue curacao and ginger liquor. Now how to bring these all together. Curacao equals citrus, then ginger and the floral notes from the vermouth.

What goes well with these? Of course, it is vanilla. Just a bit of apple to mellow out the alcohol and this is what you get. Wow this is a very strong drink.

Option 2. is for those who want it a little more mellow.

Ingredients

30 ml vanilla flavoured white spirit
15 ml white vermouth
20 ml blue curacao
10 ml ginger liquor
5 ml lime juice
30 ml apple juice

Method

Place all ingredients in a shaker and shake.

Option 1.

Strain into a chilled martini glass. Garnish with lime rind or dehydrated lime.

Option 2.

Strain into a tall glass with ice and fill with soda water. Garnish with lime wedges.

WHISKEY PEACH MULE

The Story and Tasting

As I've said before whiskey and bourbon work well with peaches. So just a little twist, adding in some ginger ale you have a good anytime drink, enjoyable for those not so sure about whiskey or bourbon. This one is helped along by the 78 Degrees Whiskey which has vanilla overtones.

Ingredients

30 ml 78 Degrees Whiskey
15 ml peach schnapps
5 ml elderflower liqueur
15 ml lime juice
Ginger beer or ale

Method

Put all ingredients in a shaker and shake with ice. Strain into tumbler with ice, top with ginger beer. Garnish with dehydrated limes and flowers.

SHIRAZ GIN SPRITZ

The Story and Tasting

It seems combining wine grapes and gin spirit is now a thing. So here's my twist on how to use these types of gins, unless you prefer it on the rocks like me.

Use gin and berries plus a bit more sparkling to add to the wine feel. Nice and refreshing and too easy to drink for a cocktail. Another one that could easily be expanded to a punch bowl or jug.

Ingredients

45 ml shiraz gin
10 ml strawberry liqueur
Splash lime juice
Strawberries
Sparkling wine

Method

Muddle a strawberry, add gin and liquor, lime juice. Shake with ice. Strain into wine glass with ice and top with sparking, garnish with a strawberry.

STUFF FROM BOTTOM OF FRIDGE

The Story and Tasting

As the name suggest this one was developed by looking at what was on the bottom shelf of the bar fridge; cachaca, grapefruit liqueur, apple and cranberry Juice. Surprising myself and the bartender I got this in one shot. No experimentation needed.

It has a slight fruity and savoury flavour at the same time.

Ingredients

10 ml Germana cachaca
30 ml silver tequila
15 ml grapefruit liqueur
30 ml apple juice
30 ml cranberry juice
15 ml lime juice
10 ml mint syrup

Method

Put all ingredients into a shaker.

Shake with ice and serve in collins glass, garnish with mint leaf and flowers.

CHRISTMAS FLIP

The Story and Tasting

Someone who had been following my cocktail endeavours asked me if I could invent a cocktail to wow participants in their Christmas cocktail event. After a bit of thought, I decided that nothing is more Christmassy than an Eggnog. And this concoction is the result. Something I really love.

We did try it with coconut milk or normal cream for those allergic to eggs, however while it was pleasant, it missed the unctuousness that the whole egg provides.

Ingredients

30 ml Kraken rum
15 ml butterscotch schnapps
15 ml ginger liqueur
10 ml sugar syrup
or
replace liqueur and syrup with
30ml ginger syrup
1 whole egg

Method

Put all ingredients into shaker and shake vigorously without ice. Add ice and shake again. Double strain into a martini glass. Dust with nutmeg.

For multiple cocktails use 2 eggs per 3 cocktails and use blender.

SPICED TROPICS RUM

The Story and Tasting

With a new rum came a new cocktail. This rum has hints of blood orange, pineapple, ginger and cinnamon, so everything I added was to enhance those flavours. Got it in one, drank it way to fast.

Ingredients

Small piece of chopped
pineapple
1-2 strawberries
depending on size
2 lychees
30 ml Reeftip Rum
15 ml Cointreau
10 ml mint syrup
30 ml apple juice

Method

Muddle pineapple, strawberry and lychees. Add other ingredients and shake. Double strain into tumbler with ice. Garnish with dehydrated pineapple and a strawberry.

EXPERIMENT 2022

The Story and Tasting

This was my first experiment for 2022, trying to use the cachaca and AGWA in different ways. Surprisingly sweet and easy drinking

Ingredients

30 ml Germana cachaca
15 ml AGWA
10 ml elderflower liqueur
15 ml lime juice
10 ml sugar syrup
30 ml apple juice

Method

Add ingredients and shake with ice. Serve in a martini glass and garnish with dehydrated apple.

NEGRONI (MULTICOLOURS)

The Story and Tasting

Here I go again wanting to change a classic. This time I was trying to get a purple coloured negroni using essentially the normal ingredients. My thinking was that red and blue make purple so why not add some blue curacao to the negroni mix. Well, we had the ratio's a little wrong and ended up with a teal colour instead.

We finally got it right by using a violet gin and mixing in the same way as my Negroni Blanco and the Negroni Viola was created.

NEGRONI TEAL

Ingredients

30 ml gin
15 ml blue curacao
30 ml rosso vermouth
15 ml Campari

Method

Add all to a large glass and stir with ice. Pour into tumbler with large ice cube. Garnish with lime peel.

NEGRONI VIOLA

Ingredients

30 ml 23rd Street Violet Gin
30 ml white vermouth
30 ml limoncello or
Cointreau

Method

Add all to a large glass and
stir with ice. Pour into
tumbler with large ice cube.
Garnish with a flower.
Add some violette liqueur
to amp the purple colour.

CRAKIN CUCUMBER

The Story and Tasting

When a local distillery produces a savoury gin (think olives, thyme, rosemary), you know I'm going to put my twisted mind to make a cocktail with it. Add some cucumber, mint and pepper – yes you have one savoury cocktail, like a really dirty martini without all the olive brine.

Wonderfully refreshing, and great with spicy or deep fried foods.

Ingredients

Cucumber pieces
Mint leaves
Cracked pepper
30 ml Threefold Mediterranean gin
15 ml mint syrup
15 ml grapefruit liqueur
30 ml apple juice

Method

Muddle cucumber, mint, and pepper. Add other ingredients and shake with ice. Double strain into martini glass, garnish with dehydrated grapefruit.

CHERRY RASPBERRIES

The Story and Tasting

With fresh berries in short supply or overly expensive, I had to look for alternatives to flavour the cocktails. I've used maraschino cherries as a garnish and the syrup in many cocktails, mainly in the *Old Fashioned* and *Manhattan*. This is the first time I've actually muddled the cherries into the cocktail. This is a very unexpected drink, not as sweet as you would imagine, really easy drinking.

Ingredients

2 maraschino cherries
2 lychees
30 ml Threefold Raspberry gin
30 ml triple sec
15 ml berry puree
Splash lime juice

Method

Muddle lychee and cherries. Mix in other ingredients and shake with ice. Double strain into martini glass.

BRASILIAN TANG

The Story and Tasting

I found out about a wonderful Brazilian rum (Cachaca), made from cane syrup instead of molasses. It's very refreshing, so why not add some more refreshing ingredients like citrus and mint?

Here you go – a very refreshing rum drink.

Ingredients

30 ml Germana Cachaca
15 ml triple sec
15 ml grapefruit liqueur
15 ml lime juice
15 ml mint syrup
30 ml apple juice

Method

Shake and serve in tumbler. Garnish with dehydrated grapefruit.